Skills in English

Level 1

Reading

Course Book

Terry Phillips

Garnet

EDUCATION

Published by
Garnet Publishing Ltd.
8 Southern Court
South Street
Reading RG1 4QS, UK

ISBN 1 85964 772 3

British Library Cataloguing-in-Publication Data
A catalogue record for this book is available from
the British Library.

Production

Project manager:	Richard Peacock
Editorial team:	Nicky Platt, Lucy Thompson, John Bates, Katharine Mendelsohn
Art director:	David Rose
Design:	Mark Slader
Illustration:	Beehive Illustration (Dave Bowyer/ Roger Wade Walker), Karen Rose, Ian West
Photography:	Corbis (Stapleton Collection/ Dennis Marsico/Wolfgang Kaehler/ Hulton-Deutsch Collection/Bettman), Digital Vision, Flat Earth, Image Source, Photodisc

Garnet Publishing wishes to thank the following for their
assistance in the development of this project:
Dr Abdullah Al Khanbashi, Abderrazak Ben Hamida,
Maxine Gillway, Glenys Roberts and the Level 1 team at
UGRU, UAE University

Every effort has been made to trace the copyright holders
and we apologize in advance for any unintentional
omissions. We will be happy to insert the appropriate
acknowledgements in any subsequent editions.

Printed and bound
in Lebanon by International Press

Contents

Book Map

Theme	Reading text type	Reading grammar	Reading skills
1 Education, Student Life	College advice leaflet	Present simple – facts Present continuous – present action Gerund as object	• Predicting content – from introduction / first paragraph • Predicting content – from headings • Word-attack skills – asking for the meaning of new words • Following instructions
2 Daily Life, Making the Most of It	Article with advice	Present simple – habits Imperative – advice	• Predicting content – from introduction / first paragraph • Predicting content – from illustrations
3 Work and Business, Are You Young and Energetic?	Job advertisement	Parts of speech	• Locating information – from headings • Dealing with new words
4 Science and Nature, Why Is It So Hot?	Popular science text	Discourse markers – exemplification	• Understanding the point of topic sentences
5 The Physical World, Big Country, Small Country	Encyclopedia articles	Present simple – facts	• Transferring information from text to chart • Skimming topic sentences for main points
6 Culture and Civilization, Fireworks, Horses and Bulls	Tourist guide information	Present simple – facts Past simple – facts	• Using chronological markers
7 They Made Our World, A Brief History of Space Travel	Magazine articles	Past simple – facts	• Using a dictionary • Recognising dates and periods
8 Art and Literature, Romeo and Macbeth	Stories from Shakespeare	Lexical cohesion	• Understanding pronoun reference
9 Sports and Leisure, Can You Play Four Army Groups?	Encyclopedia articles	Referring back: *then / there*	• Active reading – predicting tense forms
10 Nutrition and Health, Eat, Drink and Be Healthy	Lecture	Revision	• Revision

Introduction

THIS COURSE IS THE READING COMPONENT of Level 1 of the *Skills in English* series. The series takes students in four levels from Elementary to Advanced level in the four skills, Listening, Speaking, Reading and Writing.

In addition, there is a remedial/false beginner course, *Starting Skills in English*, for students who are not ready to begin Level 1.

The reading component at each level is designed to build skills that help students survive in an academic institution where reading research is wholly or partly in English.

This component can be studied on its own or with one or more of the other components, e.g., Listening and Writing.

The course is organised into themes, e.g., *Science and Nature, Art and Literature*. The same theme is used across the four skills. If, therefore, you are studying two or more components, the vocabulary and structure that you learn or practise in one component will be useful in another component.

Within each theme there are four lessons:

Lesson 1: *Vocabulary*
In the first lesson, you revise words from the theme that you have probably learnt already. You also learn some new words that you need to understand the texts in the rest of the theme.

Lesson 2: *Reading*
In this lesson, you practise skills that you have learnt in previous themes.

Lesson 3: *Learning new skills*
In this lesson, you learn one or more new skills to help you with reading.

Lesson 4: *Applying new skills*
In the final lesson, you use your new skills with another reading text. In most cases, the texts in Lesson 2 and 4 have a similar structure, so you can check that your skills have improved.

www.skillsinenglish.com

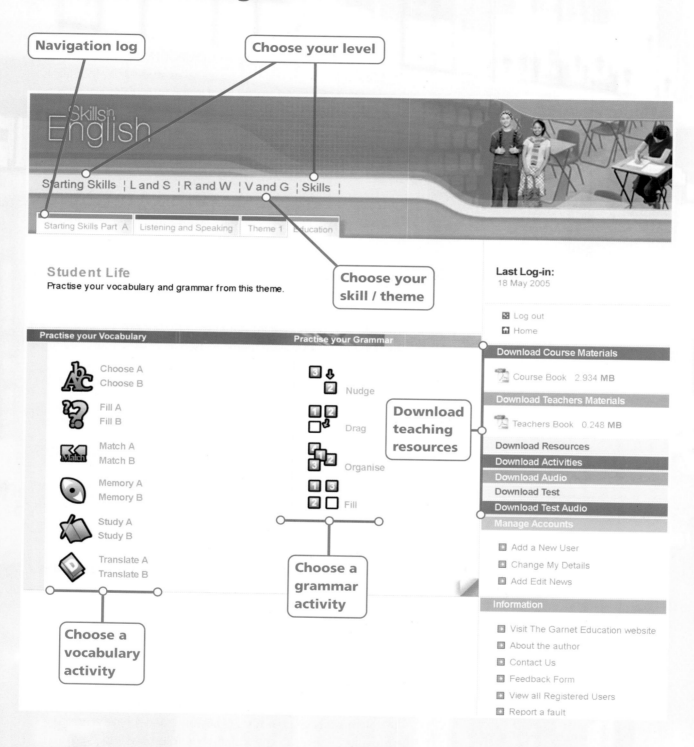

Navigation log

Choose your level

Skills in English

Starting Skills | L and S | R and W | V and G | Skills

Starting Skills Part A | Listening and Speaking | Theme 1 | Education

Student Life
Practise your vocabulary and grammar from this theme.

Choose your skill / theme

Last Log-in:
18 May 2005

Log out
Home

Practise your Vocabulary

Choose A
Choose B

Fill A
Fill B

Match A
Match B

Memory A
Memory B

Study A
Study B

Translate A
Translate B

Practise your Grammar

Nudge

Drag

Organise

Fill

Download teaching resources

Download Course Materials
Course Book   2.934 MB

Download Teachers Materials
Teachers Book   0.248 MB

Download Resources
Download Activities
Download Audio
Download Test
Download Test Audio
Manage Accounts

Add a New User
Change My Details
Add Edit News

Information

Visit The Garnet Education website
About the author
Contact Us
Feedback Form
View all Registered Users
Report a fault

Choose a grammar activity

Choose a vocabulary activity

Contact enquiries@garneteducation.com to obtain a password for access to full site information.

In this theme you are going to read a college leaflet with advice for new students.

Lesson 1: Vocabulary

You are going to learn some of the vocabulary you will need to understand the leaflet.

A Look up any red words that you don't know in a dictionary.

B Look at the green words for one minute. Then cover the words and try to remember how to complete each word below. Write the missing letters.

1 advi_____
2 assign_____
3 consid_____

4 advis_____
5 intellig_____
6 poli_____

7 rela_____
8 respe_____
9 instruct_____

C Look at this paragraph. The green words may be new to you. Read the paragraph and think: 'What does this word mean?' Then match each word to its dictionary definition.

> The instructor gave me a bad mark for my assignment. She was very polite, but she said, 'Your work was good but it was two weeks late.' I went to the student advisor. She considered the situation for a moment. Then she gave me some good advice. She said, 'Stop worrying. Relax. There is nothing wrong with your intelligence. You can get good marks. But you must respect the college rules. Don't be late with your assignments.'

1 advice   **a** an idea about a good thing to do in a particular situation
2 assignment   **b** not rude
3 consider   **c** a person who gives advice
4 advisor   **d** a piece of homework for college
5 intelligence   **e** stop working, have a break from activity
6 polite   **f** a teacher at a college or university
7 relax   **g** the ability to understand many things
8 respect   **h** think about
9 instructor   **i** think about another person's feelings when you do something

D Discuss these questions in pairs.
1 Who do you go to for *advice*?
2 How do you *relax*?
3 Which person in your life do you *respect* most?

Word list (sidebar)

answer (n and v)
ask (v)
begin (v)
dictionary (n)
end (v)
explain (v)
history (n)
learn (v)
listen (v)
mathematics (n)
question (n)
read (v)
right (adj)
science (n)
spell (v)
student (n)
study (v)
teach (v)
test (n and v)
university (n)
write (v)
wrong (adj)
advice (n)
advisor (n)
assignment (n)
consider (v)
instructor (n)
intelligence (n)
polite (adj)
relax (v)
respect (n and v)

Lesson 2: Reading

A Look quickly at the leaflet on pages 4 and 5 of the Reading Resources book. Choose the best answer to each question.

1 Who wrote the leaflet? a student OR an instructor?

2 Who is the leaflet for? new students OR old students?

3 What is in the leaflet? information OR advice?

4 How many questions are there? six OR seven?

B Look at the introduction on page 4 of the Reading Resources book.

1 Find and underline the words and phrases in a–g below.

2 Read the questions and try to understand the words and phrases.

3 Then match the words and phrases with their opposites.

a away from (home)	**1** stupidly
b sharing (a bedroom)	**2** a few
c harder	**3** old
d a lot of	**4** at (home)
e early	**5** having your own (bedroom)
f sensibly	**6** easier
g new	**7** late

C Look at Skills Check 2.

1 Read the Skills Check.

2 Cover the Skills Check.

3 Number the actions in the yellow box in order.

4 Uncover the Skills Check. Check your answer.

> ___ Think: 'What information will be in the text?'
> ___ Stop.
> ___ Read the **introduction** or **first paragraph**.

Skills Check 2

Preparing to read (1)

Read the **introduction** or **first paragraph**. Stop. Think: 'What information will be in the text?'

D Read the introduction again. It is on page 4 of the Reading Resources book.

What information will be in the next part of the leaflet?

E Barbara Peters is a new student at Greenhill College.
Look at Barbara's answers to the questions.
Work in groups. Think of advice for her.

Barbara

Lesson 3: Learning new skills

A Match each verb with a word or phrase.

1	share	**a**	at home
2	work	**b**	bed
3	make	**c**	classes
4	eat	**d**	friends
5	go to	**e**	hard
6	understand	**f**	paragraphs
7	read	**g**	a room
8	live	**h**	sensibly

B What advice did you give Barbara (Lesson 2)? Why?

C Read the introduction to the leaflet again (pages 4 and 5 of the Reading Resources book). Look at Barbara's answers to the questions. Which advice paragraphs should she read? (Don't read the paragraphs yet.)

D Read the Skills Check. Answer the questions.
1 Why don't you always have to read everything in a text?
2 How can you find out which parts to read?

E Look at the introduction to the leaflet again.
1 Answer the questions. Put ✓ or ✗ in the column 'Me'.
2 Which paragraphs should you read?

F Which paragraphs should your partner read? Ask and answer the questions in pairs.

> Are you living away from home for the first time?

> Yes, I am.

> Do you go to bed early?

> No, I don't. I often go to bed really late.

Skills Check

Preparing to read (2)

Do I have to read it all?
Sometimes you have to read **everything** in a text. But sometimes only **a few parts** are important to you. Look at the **introduction** to a text carefully to find out **which parts** of the text you have to read.

G In the left column below are the paragraph headings for the **Advice** part of the leaflet. Find a sentence on the right from each paragraph.

1 College life means … living away from home.	**a** Always ask before you borrow things from your roommate.
2 College life means … sharing a room.	**b** Don't worry if you don't have any friends at first.
3 College life means … working harder.	**c** Don't worry if you find college work hard at first.
4 College life means … making new friends.	**d** Eat sensibly.
5 College life means … taking care of yourself.	**e** If you don't understand something the first time, you can ask your instructor.
6 College life means … having a second chance.	**f** You are responsible for managing your time now.

Lesson 4: Applying new skills

A What is the opposite of the following words?
1 late _____
2 easier _____
3 a few _____
4 at home _____
5 share _____
6 stupidly _____
7 new _____

B You are going to read some, or all, of the text in **Advice** in the leaflet on pages 4 and 5 of the Reading Resources book.
1 Look at the questions in the introduction. Then look at your answers. Make a note of the paragraphs you have to read.
2 Read the correct paragraphs for you.

C Find other people who have read the same paragraphs. Ask about new words or expressions. Read the Skills Check to find ways to do this.

D Your teacher will give you a problem and a piece of advice. But the problem does not go with the piece of advice. Find a piece of advice for your problem.

E What do you think of the advice? Work in groups. Is the advice good, or can you think of something better?

Skills Check

Dealing with new words (2)

You read new words every day. Ask your teacher to explain new words. It helps you to increase your vocabulary. Here are some ways to ask:

- What's an *assignment*?
- What does *respect* mean?
- Does *polite* mean the opposite of *rude*?
- Is *intelligence* the same as *cleverness*?

I'm living away from home for the first time.

Well, you are responsible now for managing your own time ...

I don't eat sensibly.

You must take care of your health ...

In this theme you are going to read two articles about making the most of your time at college.

Lesson 1: Vocabulary

You are going to learn some vocabulary you will need to understand the articles.

A Look up any red words that you don't know in a dictionary.

B Look at the green words and phrases for one minute. Then cover the words and phrases. Try to remember how to complete each word below. Write the missing letter.

1 regula___	**4** socia___
2 weeken___	**5** brea___
3 spen___	**6** weekl___

C Find a green word or phrase for each dictionary definition.
  1 It's the opposite of *late*.
  2 It means the same as a *rest*.
  3 It's Thursday and Friday in most of the Arab World.
  4 It means *use* – time, money, energy.
  5 It's the time when you meet friends and enjoy yourself.
  6 It means *normal, usual;* something that happens at the same time each day, week or month.

D Check your answers to Exercise C in a dictionary.

E Discuss these questions in pairs.
  1 What do you do regularly every week?
  2 How much time do you spend on exercise each week?
  3 How do you usually spend the weekend?
  4 Are you usually on time for things?
  5 Which comes first, college work or your social life?

afternoon (n)
autumn (n)
day (n)
evening (n)
first (adj)
hour (n)
last (adj)
late (adj)
later (adj)
midnight (n)
minute (n)
month (n)
morning (n)
night (n)
noon (n)
now (adv)
o'clock (adv)
past (n and adv)
quarter (n)
spring (n)
summer (n)
time (n)
today (n)
tomorrow (n)
tonight (n)
week (n)
winter (n)
year (n)
yesterday (n)
break (n)
on time (prep)
regular (adj)
regularly (adv)
social life (n)
spend (v)
weekend (n)
weekly (adv)

Lesson 2: Reading

Ⓐ Complete these phrases from Theme 1. Write one word for each phrase.
1 share a _____
2 live away from _____
3 make new _____
4 eat junk _____
5 take care of _____
6 have a second _____

Ⓑ Give advice to a new student at college. Use some of the phrases in Exercise A.

Ⓒ How do you prepare to read?
1 Read the Skills Check.
2 Cover the Skills Check.
3 Write the three verbs, in order.
4 Uncover the Skills Check. Check your answer.

Ⓓ You are going to read an article from a magazine. Read the title. Answer these questions.
1 What will the article be about?
2 What will the article probably contain – facts, ideas, opinions or advice?

Ⓔ There is a diagram with this article. Look at the diagram.
1 Describe it.
2 Can you think of examples of each type of activity?
  • personal care
  • college work
  • family responsibilities
  • social life

Ⓕ 'Your weekly schedule' points to the centre of the diagram? Why? Work in groups. What do you think the article is going to say?

Your weekly schedule

College News 21 January Issue 345

College Life Is Not Just College Work

You are an adult now. You make your

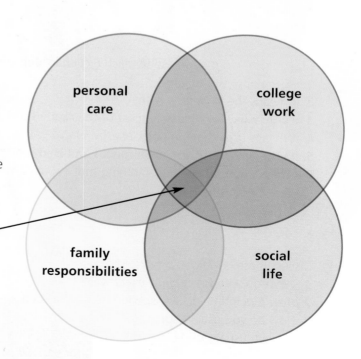

Lesson 3: Learning new skills

A Make phrases from the previous lesson with these words.

care college family life work personal
responsibilities schedule social weekly

B The phrases below are in the magazine article that you are going to read.

1 Match each phrase to one of the phrases that you made in Exercise A.
   a doing assignments _____
   b enjoying yourself _____
   c helping family members _____
   d looking after yourself _____
2 Read the first part of the article on page 6 of the Reading Resources book and check your ideas.

C Read the Skills Check. Look at the article in the Reading Resources book. Find:
   1 the title.
   2 the illustration.
   3 the introduction or first paragraph.

D Read the whole article. Choose the best summary.
   1 Some areas of your life are very important. You must make sure you do those things first.
   2 You don't have enough time to do everything, so just do the important things.
   3 You must find time for things in all these areas of your life.
   4 College work is more important than social life, family responsibilities and personal care.

E Read the article again. Close the Reading Resources book. Can you remember a phrase beginning with each verb / verb phrase below?
   1 looking after   6 have
   2 doing   7 take
   3 keeping in   8 get enough
   4 helping   9 attend
   5 enjoying   10 revise

F Work in pairs. Ask and answer the questions in the check list on page 6 of the Reading Resources book. Is your partner neglecting one area of his / her life?

Lesson 4: Applying new skills

A Think of a suitable verb to complete each expression.

1 _____ regular meals
2 _____ assignments on time
3 _____ friends regularly
4 _____ in touch
5 _____ exercise regularly
6 _____ all classes
7 _____ at the weekend
8 _____ time with the family
9 _____ enough sleep
10 _____ for tests
11 _____ yourself
12 _____ after yourself

B You are going to read another article about college life. On the right you can see the title, the introduction and the illustrations.

1 What should you do before you read the main part of the article?
2 Follow your own advice for one minute.
3 Close your book and tell your partner what the article is about. Make a list of points you expect to find in the article.

C Read the article on page 7 of the Reading Resources book. Check your list of ideas from Exercise B3.

D True or false? Explain your answers.

1 The writer of the article is an instructor.
2 The ideas in the article are the writer's own ideas.
3 He calls it his FAST way because you can do it quickly.
4 *Mentor* is another name for *college instructor*.
5 Mentors can tell you good things to do.
6 The writer says you must drive on the right road.
7 The writer says it is very bad to miss a target.
8 The writer says you can succeed without working hard.
9 *Take a break* means *have a rest*.

E Work in groups. Think of another piece of advice to add to the four-point plan.

College News   28 January   Issue 346

Making the Most of Your College Years

What did your parents say before you left for college? If your parents are like mine, they said: 'Make the most of college. It's the best time of your life.' Perhaps they are right, but how do you make the most of college?

In this theme you are going to read advertisements for work experience jobs.

Lesson 1: Vocabulary

You are going to learn some vocabulary you will need to understand the advertisements.

A Look up any red words that you don't know in a dictionary.

B Study the first extract from a dictionary. Then complete each sentence with one of the words.

1 A good _____ looks after all the people in the company.

2 If you learn many skills at college, you will be _____ when you leave.

3 That company has 200 _____ in its main office.

4 We would like to _____ you to work as a teacher.

5 What is the length of _____ in this job? I mean, how long do you want me for?

C Study the other extracts from a dictionary. Then guess the meaning of these words and phrases.

1 requirements
2 benefits
3 career-entry job

D Employers require qualifications and experience.

1 Do you have any qualifications?

2 Do you have any work experience?

Explain your answers.

---

employ (v) to pay someone to do a job

employable (adj) easy to employ, an ~ person has a lot of useful skills for an employer

employee (n) a person who is paid to do a job

employer (n) a person or company who pays someone to do a job

employment (n) **1** employing or being employed **2** a person's job

benefit (v) to get something good from, e.g., a job

career (n) several jobs in one field, e.g., teacher to senior teacher to director of education

enter (v) go into, e.g., a building

entry (n) a way to go in to, e.g., a building; a career

require (v) need

Skills Check

Learning words

When you learn a useful word, write it in your vocabulary notebook. Add other words when you learn them.

---

company (n)

computer (n)

desk (n)

e-mail (n)

envelope (n)

factory (n)

file (n)

job (n)

letter (n)

manager (n)

office (n)

secretary (n)

shelf / shelves (n)

shop (n)

start (v)

supermarket (n)

typist (n)

website (n)

work (n and v)

working hours (n)

benefit (n)

career (n)

employ (v)

employable (adj)

employee (n)

employer (n)

employment (n)

experience (n)

qualification (n)

requirement (n)

Lesson 2: Reading

Ⓐ Think of a job you would like to do when you leave college. Answer these questions.
1 What *qualifications* do you need?
2 What *experience* do you need?
3 Are there any other *requirements*, e.g., age?
4 What are the *benefits* of the job?

Ⓑ What should you look at before you read a text in detail? Complete the words.
1 the illust _____
2 the ti _____
3 the intro _____ or first _____

Ⓒ All the items on the right are from the same text. Is this text:
1 a newspaper report?
2 a leaflet?
3 an advertisement?

Ⓓ Look at all the items again.
1 Label items A–C with words from Exercise B.
2 What are the items labelled D?
3 Read the Skills Check and check your answer to D2, above.

Ⓔ Which question will each section answer? Match the questions to section headings a–f.
1 How long can I work for? ____
2 How much money do I earn? ____
3 What are the hours of work? ____
4 What jobs are available? ____
5 How old must I be? ____
6 What qualifications do I need? __C__

Ⓕ Read the text on page 8 of the Reading Resources book. Find the answers to the questions in Exercise E.

Ⓖ Read the text again.
1 Underline any new words.
2 Ask the teacher about the new words.

Ⓗ Discuss these questions in groups.
1 Could you work for Get Set this summer? Explain your answer.
2 Would you like to do a work experience course in the summer? If so, in which field?

A

Get Set
WORK EXPERIENCE COMPANY

B

We are looking for students for work experience jobs this summer.

C

D a **The Jobs**

b **Length of Employment**

c **Requirements**

d **Benefits**

e **Work**

f **Schedule**

Skills Check

Preparing to read (3)

Many texts have **section headings**. A section heading is a title for part of the text.
Always read the section headings before you read the text. Think …
What question(s) will this section answer?

Lesson 3: Learning new skills

A Study the sentences in the yellow box.
1. Do you understand the words in red?
2. Read Skills Check 1.
3. Read the sentences again. Follow the advice in the Skills Check. Do you understand the sentences?

> **a** You normally work a five-day week.
> **b** You can occasionally do overtime at the weekend.
> **c** You get additional money for this work.
> **d** Conversely, you cannot do overtime in a career-entry job.

B Study the groups of words in the green box.
1. What is the connection between each group?
2. Read Skills Check 2. Write a heading for each group of words.
3. Add more words to each group.

start	hotel	different
end	restaurant	interesting
do	job	early
get	engineering	late
must be	experience	full-time

C Study the sentences in the blue box.
1. Underline the nouns, circle the verbs and box the adjectives.
2. Read Skills Check 3 and check.

> **a** You must be in full-time education.
>
> **b** You receive extra money for this work.
>
> **c** You can do overtime at weekends.
>
> **d** They last through the summer.

Lesson 4: Applying new skills

A You are going to read another text about work experience.

   1 What should you look at before you read the text? Make a list.

   2 Find all the items on the right

B Look at the section headings. Which section will answer questions about:

accommodation?	requirements?
types of job?	money?
dates?	hours of work?

C These sentences are from the same text. Can you understand the sentences without the red words?

   1 We are looking for young, energetic people.

   2 We offer work experience jobs in many fields.

   3 We put students in schools, legal offices and police stations.

   4 They work as teachers, clerks and police cadets.

   5 You get a completion certificate.

D Study each red word in Exercise D. Is it a noun, a verb or an adjective?

E Read the text on page 9 of the Reading Resources book. Find one piece of information about each area in Exercise B. Go straight to the correct section.

Example: **accommodation:**

full-time workers get free accommodation

F Some friends are interested in work experience this summer. Can they get jobs at *The Work Experience Centre*?

   1 Juri is 18. She is studying Law. She wants to work in a legal office.

   2 Armand is 20. He is not at college. He wants to be a policeman.

   3 Barbara is 19. She is studying Education. She wants to work as a teacher.

   4 Vicente is 21. He is studying Education. He wants to get experience as a legal clerk.

   5 Aisha is 20. She is studying Law. She wants to work as a legal clerk. She can only work in July.

A The **Work Experience** Centre

B
- Do you want to earn some money this summer?
- Do you want to get useful experience for your future career?

D **a** What do we need?

b When do we need you?

c What do YOU need?

d What do you get?

e When do you work?

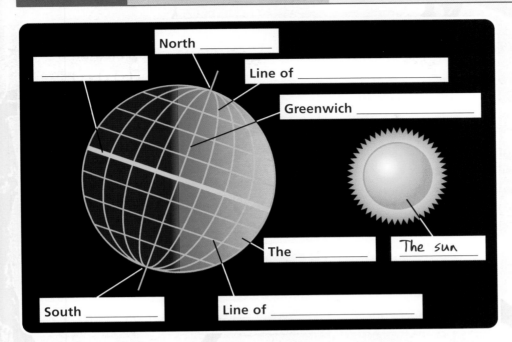

black *(adj)*
blue *(adj)*
brown *(adj)*
cloud *(n)*
cold *(adj)*
colour *(n and v)*
flower *(n)*
fog *(n)*
forest *(n)*
grass *(n)*
green *(adj)*
grey *(adj)*
hot *(adj)*
island *(n)*
lake *(n)*
mountain *(n)*
orange *(adj)*
rain *(n and v)*
red *(adj)*
river *(n)*
sea *(n)*
sky *(n)*
snow *(n and v)*
sun *(n)*
temperature *(n)*
thunderstorm *(n)*
tree *(n)*
water *(n)*
weather *(n)*
white *(adj)*
wind *(n)*
yellow *(adj)*
column *(n)*
latitude *(n)*
longitude *(n)*
meridian *(n)*
pole *(n)*
row *(n)*
source *(n)*
the Earth *(n)*
the Equator *(n)*

In this theme you are going to read two articles about the effects of the sun.

Lesson 1: Vocabulary

You are going to learn some vocabulary you will need to understand the articles.

A Look up any red words you don't know in a dictionary.

B Look at the diagram. Read the text. Label the diagram with the green words.

> Where is Abu Dhabi? We can use lines of latitude and longitude to give the position of a place on the Earth. Lines of latitude run around the Earth. The best-known line of latitude is the Equator, which runs around the centre of the Earth. Lines of longitude run from the North Pole to the South Pole. The most important line of longitude is the Greenwich Meridian, which runs through London. International time, or GMT, is taken from this line. So where is Abu Dhabi? It is on latitude 24° North and longitude 54° East.

C Look at the table. Answer the questions.
1 How many columns are there?
2 How many rows are there?
3 In which row are the column headings?
4 What does this table show?
5 What is the unit of measurement for this table?
6 Which of these cities has the highest average rainfall?
7 Which has the lowest?
8 Where does this information come from?

columns

Table 1: Average rainfall in selected capital cities	
Capital cities	Average rainfall (in mm)
Muscat	75
Abu Dhabi	42
Doha	81
Manama	77
Baghdad	400
Kuwait	115
Damascus	140

rows

Source: worldweather.com

Lesson 2: Reading

A What do tables of information have? Complete the words.

1 col_____
2 r_____
3 head_____
4 a so_____
5 a u_____ (e.g. degrees)

B Look at the table. True or false?

1 There are four columns in this table.
2 There are seven rows in this table.
3 In the first row, there are headings.
4 In the first column, there are capital cities.
5 In the second column, there is information about average rainfall.
6 All the information in this table comes from worldweather.com.
7 Muscat has the highest average temperature of these capital cities.
8 Damascus has the lowest average temperature in the world.

C The table illustrates the information in the text on page 10 of the Reading Resources book.

1 Which of these sentences do you expect to find in the text? Explain your answers.

a As you travel north or south from the Equator, the average temperature falls.
b Cities are often much warmer in summer …
c In Muscat on July 1st, sunrise is at 5.22 …
d Kampala is almost on the Equator.
e Muscat is 2,500 kilometres north of the Equator …
f The sun rises in the east …
g There are many factors that affect the average temperature.

2 Look quickly through the text on page 10 and check your answers.

D Read the text. Deal with any new words.

E Complete this summary. Use words from the text.

There are many _____ that affect average temperature, but the _____ factor is _____ from the Equator. Places near the Equator are _____ because the sun is _____ in the sky during the day.

Why Is It So Hot?

Table 1:
Average temperature in selected capital cities

Capital cities	Average temperature (in °C)	Line of latitude °N	Distance from the Equator (in km)
Muscat	28.6	23	2,530
Abu Dhabi	27.1	24	2,640
Doha	26.6	25	2,750
Manama	26.1	26	2,860
Kuwait	25.6	29	3,190
Baghdad	22.7	33	3,630
Damascus	17.0	33	3,630

Source: Average temperature information from worldweather.com

Why are some places hotter than other places? Is there one single factor that affects the average temperature at a location? The simple answer is no.

Lesson 3: Learning new skills

Ⓐ Complete these sentences from the text in Lesson 2 with one word in each space.

1 Why do some cities have a high average temperature and _____ cities have a _____ average temperature?

2 Is there one single _____ that _____ the temperature at a _____?

3 _____, there is one _____ that strongly _____ the average _____.

Ⓑ Read Skills Check 1.

1 What do you often find in a text after a statement of fact?

2 What do you often find after the word *include*?

Ⓒ Look again at the article *Why Is It So Hot?* on page 10 of the Reading Resources book. Find three sentences with examples.

Ⓓ Read Skills Check 2.

1 Find and underline the topic sentences in the article *Why Is It So Hot?*

2 Close your Reading Resources book. There is one mistake in each topic sentence in the green box. Find and correct the mistakes. Then look again at the article and check.

> **a** There are two factors that affect the average temperature.
>
> **b** However, there is one main factor that strongly influences the average rainfall.
>
> **c** As you travel north or south from the Equator, the average temperature rises.
>
> **d** Why is it so cold at the Equator?

Ⓔ Topic sentences help you predict the content of a paragraph.

1 Close your Reading Resources book again. Read the topic sentences in Exercise D. What information comes after each sentence? Discuss in pairs.

2 Look again at the article and check.

Skills Check 1

Giving examples

Many paragraphs have this structure:

statement of fact then	*As you travel north or south from the Equator, the average temperature falls.*
example(s)	*In Muscat, for example, ...*

We introduce examples with:
For example / instance, ...
Take ..., for example / instance

We introduce several examples with *include*:
There are many factors.
*These factors **include** ...*

Skills Check 2

Topic sentences

The first paragraph helps you predict the content of the text.
The **first sentence** of each paragraph often helps you predict **the content of the paragraph**.
The first sentence of a paragraph is called the **topic sentence**.

We can often use the topic sentences to make a **summary** of a text.

Lesson 4: Applying new skills

A Find pairs of words. Explain your choices.

column	high	low	many	north
one	other	some	south	row

B The items on the right all come from the same article. After each activity below, stop and think: *What will the article be about?* Discuss with your partner.
1 Read the title. (Stop, think, discuss)
2 Look at the table. (Stop, think, discuss)
3 Read the introduction – the first paragraph. (Stop, think, discuss)
4 Read the topic sentences in paragraphs 2–5. (Stop, think, discuss)

C Read the article on page 11 of the Reading Resources book straight through.
1 Underline any new words.
2 Do any of your underlined words mean the following?
   a how far
   b a line of longitude
   c not straight
   d a little bit
   e in fact
3 Look up any other underlined words in a dictionary.

D Read the article again and answer the questions.
1 This text answers a question. What is the question?
2 Which two factors affect the time of sunrise?
3 Why is sunrise later in Damascus than in Muscat?
4 Why is sunrise earlier in Tehran than in Abu Dhabi?

E Discuss in groups.
1 What do you often or always do before sunrise?
2 What do you often or always do after sunset?
3 Imagine you live in a country where sunrise is earlier and sunset is later. How does this affect your life?

Why Is It Still Dark?

Table 1:
Sunrise on July 1st in selected capital cities

Capital cities	Sunrise on July 1st	Line of longitude °E	Distance from Greenwich longitude (in km)
Muscat	5.22	59	6,490
Abu Dhabi	5.40	54	5,940
Doha	5.44	52	5,610
Manama	5.48	51	5,720
Kuwait City	6.00	48	5,280
Baghdad	6.12	45	4,950
Damascus	6.48	36	3,960

Source: Sunrise times from worldtime.com

People who travel in winter from the Gulf to London are often surprised that the sun does not rise in London until 7.30 or 8.00. Why does the sun rise at different times in different places?

There are two factors that affect the time of sunrise.

The sun rises in the east.

The second factor that affects sunrise time is the distance from the Equator.

In this theme you are going to read two encyclopedia articles about countries.

Lesson 1: Vocabulary

You are going to learn some of the vocabulary you will need to understand the articles.

Ⓐ Find red words to go in each group below. Check the meaning of the **green** words in a dictionary if necessary.
1 Features of a **landscape**
2 The **location** of something
3 Points of the **compass**

Ⓑ Read the text. Label the diagram above.

What is **the Middle East**? It is a **region** of the world. It contains many Arab countries, from Egypt in the west to Iraq in the east, and from Yemen in the south to Syria in the north.

The United Arab Emirates is one of the countries in the region. It is located between **latitude** 22° and 26° North and **longitude** 51° and 56° East. What does this mean? Lines of latitude run east to west around the world. The most important line of latitude is **the Equator**. This line is latitude 0°. Lines of longitude run north to south around the world. The most important line of longitude is the Greenwich meridian. The line runs through the city of London. This line is longitude 0°.

Ⓒ Look at the Skills Check.
1 Read the Skills Check.
2 Study the sketches.
3 Make sketches of some of the red and green words from this lesson.

Skills Check

Dealing with new words

Make sketches of new words to help you remember the meaning.

behind *(prep)*

between *(prep)*

corner *(n)*

country *(n)*

east *(n)*

in front of *(prep)*

in the centre of *(prep)*

island *(n)*

lake *(n)*

left *(n)*

mountain *(n)*

near *(prep)*

next to *(prep)*

north *(n)*

opposite *(prep)*

right *(n)*

river *(n)*

sea *(n)*

south *(n)*

town *(n)*

west *(n)*

compass *(n)*

landscape *(n)*

latitude *(n)*

location *(n)*

longitude *(n)*

region *(n)*

the Middle East *(n)*

Lesson 2: Reading

A Prepare to read the text.

1 Look at the map on the right. Which countries can you see on the map?

2 Find the headings at the bottom of the page. Are any of these words new to you? Look them up in a dictionary.

3 Read the first paragraph of the text and then read the topic sentences. What information will you read about in this text?

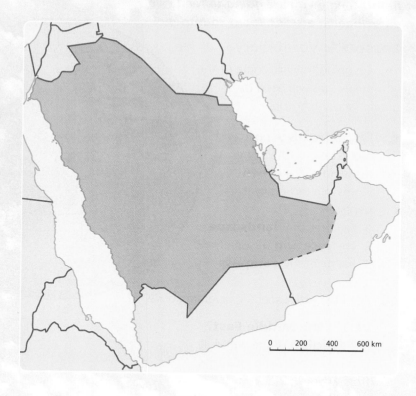

B Here are some sentences from the text you are going to read. Which paragraph does each one come from?

1 The highest point of these mountains is Jebel Sawda …

2 It occupies the majority of the Arabian peninsula.

3 To the south, it is bordered by Yemen and Oman.

4 There is another large city, Jeddah, on the Red Sea.

5 There are two large sand deserts.

C Look quickly at the text on page 12 of the Reading Resources book. Check your answers to Exercise B.

D Read the text.

1 Deal with any new words.

2 Mark all the places mentioned on the map.

E Match the verbs and the other words to make phrases from the text.

1 occupies	**a** a height of 3,133 metres
2 is located	**b** a long coastline on the Red Sea
3 covers	**c** an area of nearly 2 million square kilometres
4 has	**d** by Jordan, Iraq and Kuwait
5 is bordered	**e** down to the Gulf in the east
6 reaches	**f** in the centre of the country
7 slopes	**g** the majority of the Arabian peninsula

Location	**Saudi Arabia is a large country situated in the region called the Middle East.** It occupies the majority of the Arabian peninsula. It is located between latitudes 16° and 32° North and longitudes 35° and 55° East.
Capital and other main cities	**The capital is Riyadh.**
Area and borders	**The country covers an area of nearly 2 million square kilometres.**
Landscape	**There are mountains along the coast in the west of the country.**

Lesson 3: Learning new skills

A Look at the words in each column.

    1 Make phrases with one word from each column.

    2 Does the phrase normally have *the*?

    Example: *the Middle East*

a Middle		**1** city	
b Arabian		**2** coastline	
c holy		**3** desert	
d Red		**4** East	
e square		**5** east	
f long		**6** kilometres	
g highest		**7** marshes	
h Rub al Khali		**8** peninsula	
i salt		**9** point	
j fresh		**10** rivers	
k south		**11** Sea	
l permanent		**12** water	

B You are going to complete a table with information from the text in Lesson 2 (page 12 of the Reading Resources book).

    1 Read the Skills Check.

    2 Which nouns in the text can you use as section headings? Find and underline possible nouns.

    3 Which other words can you change to nouns and use as headings?

C Read the information in each section of the table below. Choose a suitable underlined noun for each section.

Country		Saudi Arabia
Region		the Middle East
		Riyadh
		Jeddah, Makkah
Location	latitude	between 16° and 32° N
		between 35° and 55° E
		nearly 2,000,000 sq km
		Jordan, Iraq, Kuwait
		Yemen, Oman
		Qatar, United Arab Emirates, the Gulf
		the Red Sea
		most of the land is sandy desert
		none, but salt marshes and swamps in the east
		Jebel Sawda (3,133 m)

D Cover the text and the table in Exercise C above. What information can you remember about Saudi Arabia? Test each other in pairs.

Lesson 4: Applying new skills

A Look at the beginnings of these words from this unit.
  1 Can you say the whole word?
  2 What does it mean?
   a peni ... *nsula*   **f** loca ...
   b lati ...   **g** regi ...
   c longi ...   **h** coa ...
   d bord ...   **i** mar ...
   e situa ...   **j** des ...

B Cover the text at the bottom right-hand side of the page. Look at the map. Discuss these points.
  1 What sort of information will be in the text?
  2 What section headings will be in the text?
  3 What specific information will be in the text? Think of five things.

C Uncover the text at the bottom of the page. Read the section headings and the topic sentences. Check your ideas from Exercise B.

D Here are some sentences from the text. Which paragraph is each one from?
  1 It lies on latitude 26° North and longitude 50° East.
  2 The land area is growing.
  3 There are no other large cities.
  4 There are no permanent rivers on any of the islands.

E Look quickly at the text on page 13 of the Reading Resources book. Check your answers to Exercise D.

F Read the text.
  1 Deal with new words.
  2 Transfer the information to a chart.

G Compare your charts in pairs.

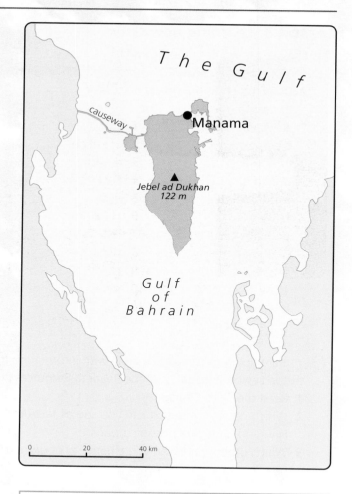

Location
Bahrain occupies 33 islands in the Gulf.

Capital and other main cities
The capital, Manama, is located on the north coast of Bahrain island.

Area
The country has an area of 665 square kilometres.

Borders
To the south and west is the Gulf of Bahrain.

Physical features
The majority of the land is stony or sandy desert.

In this theme you are going to read two magazine articles about traditional events.

Lesson 1: Vocabulary

You are going to learn some of the vocabulary you will need to understand the articles.

A Look at the red words for one minute. Then cover the words and try to remember the word(s) beginning:

a…	d…	l…	o…	th…
b…	f…	m…	p…	w…
c…	g…	n…	s…	

B Read the text. Then write a green word in each space in the table.

Guy Fawkes Night is a traditional event in England. It takes place every year on November 5th. The event started in 1607. Two years earlier, a man called Guido (or Guy) Fawkes tried to blow up the Houses of Parliament. He failed. Now, every year, people celebrate.

For weeks before the event, people build big piles of wood in the fields. On the day of the event, some children dress up like Guy Fawkes. In the evening, everyone goes to a local field and someone lights the big fire. Then there are fireworks. After that, people have dinner – usually sausages and burgers nowadays!

Where does the _____ take place?	England
What is it called?	Guy Fawkes Night
When does it _____?	On November 5th.
When did the event first begin?	In 1607.
What does the event _____?	People are happy because Guy Fawkes failed.
How do people _____ for the event?	They build big piles of wood.
Do people wear _____ clothes?	Yes – children dress up as Guy Fawkes.
What _____ on the day?	There is a big fire and fireworks.
What happens after the event?	People have dinner.

Vocabulary list:

adult (n)
age (n)
be born (v)
boy (n)
child (n)
congratulations (n)
dead (adj)
die (v)
family (n)
friend (n)
girl (n)
group (n)
guest (n)
live (v)
man (n)
married (adj)
name (n)
old (adj)
party (n)
people (n)
person (n)
present (n)
single (adj)
thank (v)
thank you (interj)
woman (n)
celebrate (v)
event (n)
happen (v)
prepare (v)
special (adj)
take place (v)
traditional (adj)

Lesson 2: Reading

A Prepare to read the text.

1 Look at the title. Name a traditional event in your country.

2 Look at the subheading. What do you think the *Palio* is? What about *Siena*?

3 Look at the map. Check your answers to question 2 above.

4 Look at the picture. Check your answers to question 2 above again.

5 Read the first paragraph. What extra information do you get?

6 Read the topic sentences. What extra information do you expect in each paragraph?

B Here are some sentences from the text. Which paragraph do you think each one comes from?

___ It only lasts 90 seconds.

___ The Black Death of 1348, however, killed thousands of people.

___ The flags belong to the 17 areas of the city.

___ Then, in the late afternoon, there is a parade in the Piazza del Campo.

___ Thousands of visitors come to the city every year just to see it.

C Look quickly at the text on page 14 of your Reading Resources book. Check your answers to Exercise B.

D Read the text. Deal with any new words. Answer these questions.

1 Where is Siena?

2 What is the Palio?

3 When was the first ever race?

4 When does the Palio take place?

5 What sort of clothes do people wear for the event?

6 When does the race start?

7 Where does it take place?

8 How many men take part?

9 How long is the race?

10 When does it finish?

E Make a table of the important information about the Palio for visitors to Italy.

A

GREAT TRADITIONAL EVENTS
∞∞∞ AROUND THE WORLD ∞∞∞

1: *The Palio in Siena*

Siena is a city of around 56,000 people. It is situated in central Italy, 65 kilometres south of Florence and 271 kilometres northwest of Rome. It is built on a high hilltop.

B Siena was once an important centre for banking and for art.

C Siena is famous today for a horse race.

D For three days before the event, flags fly from houses and shops.

E On the day of the event, the young men and women of the city dress up in colourful clothes from the Middle Ages.

F Finally, at exactly 6.30 p.m., the race begins.

Lesson 3: Learning new skills

A Which words from Lesson 2 mean ...
1 a square in an Italian town?
2 an old disease?
3 a person who rides a horse in a race?
4 people walking together for a festival, usually wearing interesting clothes?
5 showing something to large groups of people?
6 a period in history?

B These adjectives and nouns appear as phrases in the text on page 14 of the Reading Resources book.
1 Match each adjective with a noun.
2 Check with the text.

a	high	1	afternoon
b	important	2	clothes
c	colourful	3	square
d	late	4	dinners
e	main	5	hilltop
f	special	6	centre

C Some prepositions (*in, at, for, of*, etc.) are missing from these sentences.
1 Complete each sentence with the missing preposition.
2 Read Skills Check 1. Check your answers.
   a (The race) takes place _____ July and August.
   b _____ three days before the event, flags fly from houses and shops.
   c _____ the day of the event, the young men and women of the city dress up.
   d _____ the morning they walk around the streets.
   e _____ the late afternoon, there is a parade in the Piazza del Campo.
   f _____ exactly 6.30 p.m., the race begins.

D Imagine you saw the Palio in Siena.
1 Read the last two paragraphs again (page 14 of the Reading Resources book).
2 Look at Skills Check 2.
3 Tell your partner about the day of the Palio.

Piazza del Campo

Lesson 4: Applying new skills

A What information does a tourist want to know about a traditional event? Write questions in the first column of the table.

Where does the event take place?	

B Look at the first paragraph and topic sentences from the text.

1 How many of the questions from Exercise A can you answer? Write answers in the second column.

2 In which paragraph do you expect to find answers to your other questions?

C Read the complete text on page 15 of the Reading Resources book. Find answers to the rest of your questions from Exercise A.

D Guess or work out the meaning of these words from context.

1 agricultural area
2 water buffalo
3 chariot
4 tail
5 coconut
6 decorate

E Imagine you saw the bull racing in Negara.

1 Read the last three paragraphs again (page 15 of the Reading Resources book).

2 Tell your partner about the day of the race.

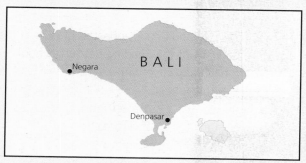

A

GREAT TRADITIONAL EVENTS

∘∘∘∘∘ AROUND THE WORLD ∘∘∘∘∘

2: *Bull racing in Bali*

Bali is a small island in Indonesia. On the western coast of the island there is a town called Negara. It has a population of around 34,000. Negara is an agricultural area. They grow coconuts and bananas there. It is about 50 km west of the capital, Denpasar.

B Bali is a popular tourist island, but for most of the year very few people go to Negara.

C The event began about 100 years ago.

D The bulls are not ordinary farm animals.

E On the day, the jockeys prepare for the race.

F The race starts!   **G** It is a strange race.

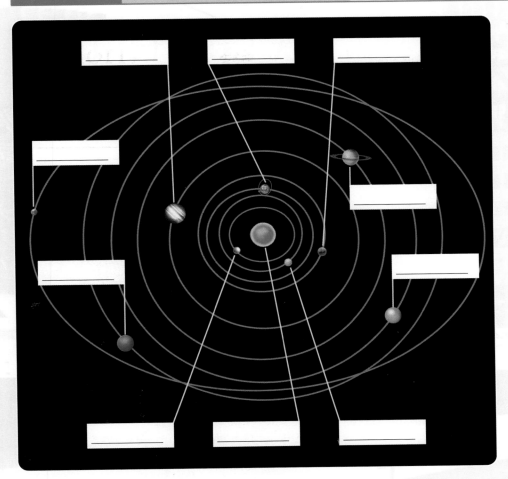

accident (n)
airport (n)
arrive (v)
bicycle (n)
boat (n)
bus (n)
bus stop (n)
car (n)
come (v)
drive (v)
driver (n)
fly (v)
go (v)
land (v)
leave (v)
passenger (n)
pilot (n)
plane (n)
road (n)
sail (v)
sailor (n)
ship (n)
street (n)
take off (v)
traffic (n)
train (n)
planet (n)
satellite (n)
solar system (n)
space (n)
star (n)
the Earth (n)
the moon (n)
the sun (n)

In this theme you are going to read two texts about the history of space travel.

Lesson 1: Vocabulary

You are going to learn some vocabulary you will need to understand the texts.

A Read the title of the unit. Which of the red words are connected with this topic?

B Read this text, which includes the green words. Label the diagram above.

> The sun is a star at the centre of our solar system. Nine planets orbit the sun. Mercury is the planet closest to the sun. Venus is the second planet. It is the hottest. The Earth is the third planet from the sun. It is the planet that we live on. It has a natural satellite, the moon. The moon orbits the Earth. Mars is the fourth planet. It is sometimes called the red planet.
>
> The next four planets are giant balls of gas. Jupiter, the fifth planet from the sun, is the largest planet in the solar system. Saturn is the sixth planet from the sun. It has large rings. Uranus is the seventh planet and Neptune is the eighth planet from the sun.
>
> Pluto is usually the furthest from the sun. It is the smallest planet. In fact, it is so small that some scientists say it is not a planet at all.

C What is the name of each object in the solar system in your language?

Lesson 2: Reading

A Prepare to read the text.

1 Look at the title. Tell your partner three facts that you know about space travel.

2 Look at the subheading. Find pictures of two of the items in the illustrations for this lesson.

3 Read the first paragraph. Answer these questions in pairs.

   a When did the Chinese first make gunpowder?

   b What can you use gunpowder for?

   c The article is about space travel. What connects gunpowder and space travel?

4 Read the topic sentences. Then read each statement below. Is it true or false? If it's false, correct it.

   a Paragraph 1 will probably be about Chinese rockets.

   b Paragraph 2 will probably be about Arab traders.

   c Paragraph 3 will also probably be about Arab traders.

   d Paragraph 4 will probably be about one man.

   e Paragraph 5 will probably be about the future.

B Read the text on page 16 of the Reading Resources book.

1 Deal with any new words – look again at the Skills Checks on pages 8, 10 and 17.

2 Check your ideas in Exercise A4 above.

C Which word or phrase in the text means …

1 people you are fighting in a war?

2 periods of 100 years?

3 very old?

4 from the Middle Ages?

5 e.g., petrol, oil?

6 gas with the symbol O?

7 Earth, Mars, Venus, etc.?

D Make a table of the information in the text.

Date	Event
c800	Chinese invented gunpowder.
c10th–c13th	

A Brief History of Space Travel

PART I

Fireworks, cannons and rockets

Fireworks

Cannon of the Middle Ages

Castle

In about 800 BCE, a Chinese person mixed sulphur (S) and potassium nitrate (KNO_3), and carbon (C). He set fire to the mixture. It exploded. The mixture was gunpowder.

[1] The Chinese mainly used the new invention in fireworks, but they also made rockets.

[2] Between the 10th and 13th centuries, Arab traders in China learnt about gunpowder.

[3] The Europeans also put gunpowder in new guns called cannons.

[4] Werner von Braun, a German scientist, studied the rockets of the ancient Chinese and the cannons of medieval Europe.

[5] On September 8th, 1944, the first rocket hit London.

Lesson 3: Learning new skills

A How many facts can you remember from the last lesson?

1 Read Skills Check 1.
2 Think of five more facts from the text in Part 1 of *A Brief History of Space Travel*.
3 Check your ideas with the text on page 16 of the Reading Resources book.

B What is the infinitive of each of these verbs from Lesson 2?

1 Write the infinitive.
2 Read Skills Check 2.
3 Use a dictionary to check your answers.

past simple	infinitive
lit	light
blew	
made	
led	
took	
put	

C What do you expect to come after these words in a text about history?

1 Match each preposition to a type of time information.

a in		**1** a day or date
b on		**2** a time period
c around		**3** a year or a month
d between		**4** an approximate date
e over		**5** two dates or time periods

2 Read Skills Check 3 and check your answers.
3 Give more examples of each type of time information.

D What are the important dates in the history of your country or your city / town? Make some past tense sentences with prepositions + time expressions from Exercise C.

Skills Check 1

Past simple for history

We use the past simple for **facts from history**.
Examples:
*In about 800 BCE, a Chinese person **mixed** three natural substances.*
*He **lit** the mixture.*
*It **blew** up.*
*The mixture **was** gunpowder.*

Skills Check 2

Using a dictionary for verbs

Look up an irregular past tense verb in a dictionary. You will find something like this:

lit /lɪt/ *past* and *past part.* of light

You must look up *light* to find the meaning.
Note: Some irregular verbs have the same form for the infinitive and the past simple. In the dictionary you will find something like this:

put /pʊt/ *vb* **puts, putting, put**

The last word in **bold** is the past simple form.

Skills Check 3

Recognising dates and periods

Writers often give **the date** or **the period** of a fact from history.
Look for these time expressions.

Year	*In 1936 …*
Month	*In December …*
Day	*On September 8th …*
Period of time	*Over 1,000 **years later** …*
	***Between the** 10th and 13th **centuries** …*

Sometimes the writer does not know the exact date.
Examples:
***Around** 800 BCE …*   OR   ***In about** 800 BCE …*

Lesson 4: Applying new skills

A Read this summary of Part 1 of *A Brief History of Space Travel*. Correct the six mistakes in the facts.

In the first part we learnt about the invention of fireworks and cannons by the ancient Japanese. Then we learnt how the Europeans brought the inventions back from China. We saw that the invention of the space rocket in Europe led to the end of castles. Finally, we met Brauner von Wern and his planets.

B You are going to read Part 2.
  1 Read the subheading. What do you expect to find in this text?
  2 Read the topic sentences. Which paragraph do you expect to answer each question below?
    ___ What did all the space journeys of the first 20 years have in common?
    ___ What did von Braun do in America?
    ___ What is an artificial satellite?
    ___ What was special about the Space Shuttle?
    ___ Who produced the first space rocket?
    ___ Who was the first American astronaut in space?

C Read the text on page 17 of the Reading Resources book. Deal with any new words. Check your answers to Exercise B.

D Which word or phrase in the text means ...
  1 a very big rocket?
  2 a man-made object that goes round the Earth?
  3 a person who goes into space?
  4 part of a space rocket that comes back to Earth?
  5 learn about?
  6 send from the Earth?
  7 to go round the sun or a planet?

E Continue the table of information you started in Lesson 2.

F Do some research. Find five more facts about space travel with dates for your *Brief History of Space Travel* table. Try www.en.wikipedia.org or www.encarta.msn.com.

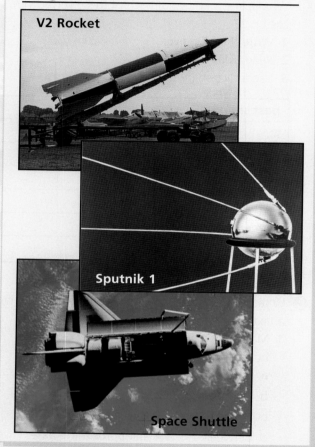

A Brief History of Space Travel

PART 2
Dogs, Men, Women and Shuttles

V2 Rocket

Sputnik 1

Space Shuttle

[A] After the war, Werner von Braun went to America.

[B] However, von Braun did not actually produce the first space rocket.

[C] Finally, in October 1957, the Russians used a rocket to send the first artificial satellite into space.

[D] Four years later, the Russian astronaut Yuri Gagarin became the first man in space.

[E] All these space journeys, and many more in the first 20 years of space travel, had one thing in common.

[F] On April 12th, 1981, the Americans launched the first Space Shuttle.

In this theme you are going to read about two of Shakespeare's plays.

Lesson 1: Vocabulary

You are going to learn some vocabulary to help you understand the texts.

Ⓐ All the red words are infinitives. Your teacher is going to show you some past tense verbs. Find and number the correct infinitive in each case.

Ⓑ What do you know about Shakespeare? Do the quiz. Choose one or more answer(s) in each case.

		A	B	C
1	What was his first name?	William	Henry	Andrew
2	When was he born?	1564	1764	1964
3	Where was he born?	London	Manchester	Stratford
4	Which university did he go to?	Oxford	Cambridge	none
5	When did he get married?	at 18	at 28	at 38
6	What was the first name of his wife?	Anne	Anna	Annie
7	How many children did he have?	1	2	3
8	Which of these plays did he write?	*Hamlet*	*Romeo and Juliet*	*Macbeth*
9	How many plays did he write?	5	35	53
10	What type of plays did he write?	funny plays	about kings and queens	sad plays

Ⓒ Read the text and check your answers to Exercise B.

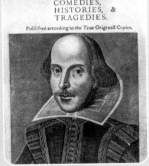

William Shakespeare was born on April 23rd, 1564. He was born in Stratford, a town in the centre of England. He is probably the most important person in English literature. However, we know very little about his childhood or early life. We do know that he did not go to university. He got married at 18 to Anne Hathaway. Their first child, Susanna, was born one year later, in May 1583. His twins were born in February 1585. He wrote his first play in 1589. It was called *Henry VI*. In 1594, he moved to London. He became an actor, but he continued to work as a playwright. He wrote 35 plays altogether. People know his characters, including Hamlet, Romeo and Juliet and Macbeth, all around the world. He wrote comedies – funny plays; histories – about the lives of kings and queens; and tragedies – plays with an unhappy ending. He died on his birthday in 1616.

Ⓓ Look at the green words. Give a definition of each word, then check with a dictionary.

bring *(v)*
build *(v)*
carry *(v)*
check *(v)*
climb *(v)*
come *(v)*
do *(v)*
draw *(v)*
end *(v)*
feel *(v)*
find *(v)*
get *(v)*
give *(v)*
go *(v)*
leave *(v)*
live *(v)*
look *(v)*
make *(v)*
meet *(v)*
move *(v)*
point *(v)*
put *(v)*
run *(v)*
say *(v)*
send *(v)*
start *(v)*
stop *(v)*
take *(v)*
talk *(v)*
tell *(v)*
walk *(v)*
want *(v)*
character *(n)*
comedy *(n)*
history *(n)*
literature *(n)*
play *(n)*
playwright *(n)*
tragedy *(n)*

Lesson 2: Reading

A Prepare to read the text.

 1 Look at the illustrations, the title and the first paragraph.

 2 Which of these sentences do you expect to find in the text? Tick one or more.
 - ☐ However, the plan went wrong.
 - ☐ Shakespeare wrote many other plays.
 - ☐ Romeo Montague fell in love with Juliet Capulet.
 - ☐ Juliet's friend had an idea.
 - ☐ William Shakespeare died in 1616.

B Read each topic sentence. What will be in the rest of the paragraph?

C Read the text on page 18 of the Reading Resources book.

 1 Check your answers to Exercise A.

 2 Check your ideas from Exercise B.

D Number the illustrations in the correct order.

E Guess the meanings of these words:

1	performances	5	body
2	hated	6	wake / woke
3	sword	7	poison
4	marriage	8	tragedy

F Tell the story of *Romeo and Juliet* in your own words.

Love Story Lasts 400 Years

Romeo and Juliet is one of the most famous tragedies in the world. William Shakespeare wrote it between 1590 and 1595. There have been thousands of performances in the 400 years since then. The story is simple and very sad.

A Romeo Montague fell in love with Juliet Capulet.

B Then something terrible happened.

C Juliet's father wanted her to marry a man called Paris.

D Juliet's friend had an idea.

E However, the plan went wrong.

F Something good came out of the tragedy.

Lesson 3: Learning new skills

A Make sentences about *Romeo and Juliet* using words from each column.
Example: *Romeo and Juliet fell in love.*

1	2	3
Romeo	didn't know	in love.
	fell	each other.
Juliet	got	a young Capulet.
	had	the city.
The Montagues	hated	married.
	killed	her to marry.
The Capulets	left	about her marriage.
	took	an idea.
Juliet's father	wanted	back to the city.
	went	poison.
Juliet's friend	came	up.
	woke	wrong.
The plan	found	Romeo dead.

B Read Skills Check 1.
   1 Find and underline regular verbs in Column 2 of Exercise A.
   2 Find and circle irregular verbs in Column 2 of Exercise A. What is the infinitive of each irregular verb?

C Read Skills Check 2.
   1 Find and underline all the pronouns in the text on page 18 of the Reading Resources book. What does each pronoun refer to?
   2 Find the phrases a–g in the text. For each of these phrases, find another word or phrase with the same meaning in the text.

a the idea		**1**	Juliet
b the accident		**2**	the plan
c your husband		**3**	Romeo
d his wife		**4**	the death of Romeo and Juliet
e the tragedy		**5**	Romeo and Juliet
f the two families		**6**	killing the young Capulet
g the two young people		**7**	the Montagues and the Capulets

   3 Cover the right column. Can you remember the other way of referring in each case?

D What have you learned in this lesson? Cover the Skills Checks and explain them in groups.

'Macbeth, King of Scotland'

'...when the trees come to Dunsinane'

Lesson 4: Applying new skills

A You are going to read about another Shakespeare play. Prepare to read the text.

B Read the text. It is on page 19 of the Reading Resources book.

1 Number the illustrations in order.

2 Find these items in the illustrations.

a castle   d tree
b king   e witch
c soldier   f wood

C Guess the meanings of these words.

1 history   5 guilt / guilty
2 Lord   6 kill
3 Lady   7 murder
4 tale   8 die

D The writer refers to the items below in different ways. Find more ways in the text for each item.

1 Macbeth   5 Dunsinane
2 Lady Macbeth 6 a wood
3 Duncan   7 an army
4 three witches 8 the murder

E Find and underline all the pronouns. What does each pronoun refer to?

F Work in pairs. What is the story of *Macbeth*? Tell the story in your own words.

Macbeth
Tragedy or History?

Shakespeare's play *Macbeth* is a tragedy in the theatre, but it is almost a history. There was a real man called Macbeth. He lived in Scotland in around 1050. Shakespeare wrote the play in about 1605. It is a tale of murder and guilt.

A| Lord and Lady Macbeth lived in a castle.

B| However, one day he met three witches.

C| Duncan came to their castle and Macbeth killed him.

D| Macbeth met the three women again.

E| Macbeth went home.

THEME 9 Sports and Leisure — Can You Play Four Army Groups?

In this theme you are going to read about two board games.

Lesson 1: Vocabulary

You are going to learn some vocabulary that you will need to understand the texts.

A Look up any red words you don't know in a dictionary.

B Cover the red words.
1 Can you recognise each word below from the first few letters? Sometimes there are several possible words.

ba...	mag...	ra...	te...
bea...	new...	sh...	th...
fi...	pl...	sp...	tu...
ho...	pro...	sw...	wa...

2 Test each other in pairs.

C Read the text. Label the illustration.

> These people are playing a game. It is a game for four players. They are using small playing pieces. They have different colours – red, blue, green and yellow. They are playing on a board with lots of squares.
>
> How do you play a game like this? The players take turns. One player moves one of his pieces – one, two or three squares, for example. Then another player has a turn. He moves one of *his* pieces. What happens if he lands on the same square? His opponent has to take his piece back to the start.
>
> The objective of this game is to get all your pieces home first. In this game, home is in the middle of the board.

D Answer these questions about the game in Exercise C.
1 How many players are there?
2 What do you call a person you are playing against?
3 How do you play the game?
4 How do you win this game?
5 Do you play this game in your country? What is it called?

Vocabulary list (red words)

ball (n)
beach (n)
film (n and v)
football (n)
hobby (n)
magazine (n)
news (n)
newspaper (n)
play (n and v)
programme (n)
radio (n)
show (n)
sport (n)
sports (n)
swimming (n)
tennis (n)
theatre (n)
turn off (v)
turn on (v)
watch (v)
game (n)
land (v)
objective (n)
piece (n)
player (n)
turn (n)

Lesson 2: Reading

A You are going to read a text about a game. Look at the illustrations from the text. Can you name any of the things?

B Look at the section headings underneath the illustrations. Which section do you need to read if you want to find out the following information?

1 How many pieces are there in the game?
2 Which country does the game come from?
3 What are the pieces called?
4 What happens at the end of the game?
5 What do the players do in the game?

C Look at the topic sentences from each section. Which section does each topic sentence come from? Write the letter next to each topic sentence. (One section has two paragraphs so it needs two topic sentences.)

D Do you know this game? Have a guess!

E Look quickly at the text on page 20 of the Reading Resources book. Check your answers to Exercise B.

F Read the text carefully. After reading each paragraph, stop and think: *What is this game?*

G We have seen that writers often use different words for the same thing. What words does the writer here use for …

1 the playing pieces?
2 the other player?
3 the game?

H Label the things in the illustrations. Use words from the text.

[A]
a) History
b) The playing pieces
c) How to play
d) How to win

[B] 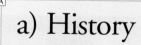 From India, it passed to Persia in the 6th century.

[C] The game is for two players.

[D] The names of the pieces show the history of the game.

[E] The objective of the game is simple.

[F] People first played this game in India over 2,000 years ago.

Lesson 3: Learning new skills

Ⓐ What information can you remember from each section of the text about chess? Work in groups.
1 History
2 The playing pieces
3 How to play
4 How to win

Ⓑ What is *active reading*?
1 What do you understand by the expression? Discuss in pairs.
2 Read the first part of Skills Check 1. Check your ideas.

Ⓒ Predicting tense forms
1 Read the rest of Skills Check 1.
2 Look back at the section headings in Exercise A. What tense forms were in each section?
3 Find each paragraph in the text on page 20 of the Reading Resources book and check your ideas.

Ⓓ Referring back
1 Look again at the text on page 20. Find and underline all the pronouns in the first two paragraphs of the text. What does each pronoun refer to?
2 Read Skills Check 2.
3 Find the words *then* and *there* in the first two paragraphs of the text. Does the word refer back in each case? Or does it introduce the next action / a new piece of information?

Ⓔ Can you play chess? Do you like it? How do some of the pieces move?

Skills Check 1

Active reading

Active reading means …
- predicting content, *then*
- reading, *then*
- comparing content with predictions.

Predicting tense forms is part of predicting content. You can usually predict the tense forms in a paragraph from …
- the heading
- the topic sentence

Examples:

Heading	Topic sentence	Tense?
Origins	*People first **played** this game in India over 2,000 years ago.*	Past simple
The playing pieces	*The names of the pieces **show** the history of the game.*	Present simple

---

Skills Check 2

Referring back

We have seen that **pronouns** refer back to previous nouns. We can use **other words** to refer back:
then = referring back to a date or time
there = referring back to a place

Examples:
Then, *they used real soldiers.* = 2,000 years ago
There, *Arab traders learned the game.* = in Persia
But be careful!
The word *then* can also introduce the next action.
The word *there* can also introduce a new piece of information.

Examples:
One player moves, **then** *the other player.*
There *are now more than 40 million players in Russia alone.*

Lesson 4: Applying new skills

You are going to read about another game.

A Read the section headings.
1 What tense do you predict for each section?
2 What information do you expect to find in each section?

B Read the topic sentences. Check / Correct your predictions.

C Read the sentences below. Which section does each sentence come from?
1 Make a prediction. Write the section letter in the box.
2 Look quickly at the text on page 21 of the Reading Resources book and check your answers.
   a ☐ A piece can move one square, diagonally, forward.
   b ☐ Each player starts with 12 pieces.
   c ☐ Five hundred years before then, it began in Egypt.
   d ☐ However, the game did not start there.
   e ☐ One player has red disks and one has white.
   f ☐ One player must take all the opponent's pieces.
   g ☐ The Arabs took the game to Spain ...
   h ☐ The pieces are all disks.
   i ☐ They dated the game to about 3,000 BCE.
   j ☐ When a piece arrives at the opponent's edge of the board, it becomes a king.
   k ☐ The first book about this new version appeared in Spain in 1547.

D Read the text carefully. After reading each paragraph, stop and …
1 think: *What game is this text about?*
2 Discuss with your partner.

E Find and underline …
1 all the pronouns.
2 *there* and *then*.
What does each word refer to?

F Can you play this game? Do you like it?

[A]
a) History
b) A new rule
c) The playing pieces
d) How to play
e) How to win

[B] Archaeologists discovered an early version of this game in the ruins of the ancient city of Ur in Iraq.

[C] The objective of the game is simple.

[D] Around 1535 in France, a new rule appeared.

[E] You play the game on a normal chessboard, with 64 black and white squares.

[F] The game is for two players.

[G] The game is mentioned in the Arabic book *Kitab-al Aghani*, which appeared sometime in the 10th century.

In this theme you are going to do a quiz and read two articles about healthy eating.

Lesson 1: Vocabulary

You are going to learn some vocabulary you will need to understand the articles.

A Find pairs of red words. Explain the connection.

Example: bottle – milk = *You can get milk in a bottle.*

B Look at the quiz.

1 Ask and answer in pairs. Tick (✔) your partner's choice in each case.

2 Tell your partner his / her score.

3 Read *Understanding your score*. Do you agree?

| **bottle** (n) |
| **bread** (n) |
| **breakfast** (n) |
| **butter** (n) |
| **cheese** (n) |
| **chicken** (n) |
| **coffee** (n) |
| **cup** (n) |
| **drink** (n and v) |
| **eat** (v) |
| **egg** (n) |
| **fish** (n) |
| **food** (n) |
| **fruit** (n) |
| **glass** (n) |
| **ice-cream** (n) |
| **jam** (n) |
| **juice** (n) |
| **meal** (n) |
| **meat** (n) |
| **menu** (n) |
| **milk** (n) |
| **restaurant** (n) |
| **rice** (n) |
| **salad** (n) |
| **salt** (n) |
| **sandwich** (n) |
| **sugar** (n) |
| **tea** (n) |
| **vegetable** (n) |
| **biscuit** (n) |
| **burger** (n) |
| **cake** (n) |
| **cereal** (n) |
| **chip** (n) |
| **chocolate** (n) |
| **crisp** (n) |
| **pasta** (n) |
| **potato(es)** (n) |
| **sweet** (n) |

Section A

1 How much butter do you have on bread?
- **a** Lots
- **b** A little
- **c** None

2 How often do you eat biscuits or cakes in a week?
- **a** 5 or more times
- **b** 2–4 times
- **c** Sometimes or never

3 How often do you eat sweets or chocolate in a week?
- **a** 5 or more times
- **b** 2–4 times
- **c** Sometimes or never

4 How often do you eat chips or crisps in a week?
- **a** 5 or more times
- **b** 2–4 times
- **c** Sometimes or never

5 How often do you eat burgers in a week?
- **a** 5 or more times
- **b** 2–4 times
- **c** Sometimes or never

How to score

A = 5 points; B = 3 points; C = 1 point

Understanding your score You need a low score for Section A. A score below 10 is very good. If you get a score of 20 or more, you need to reduce the amount of sugar and fat in your diet. You need a high score for Section B. A score of 20 or over is very good. If you get a score of 10 or less, you need to increase the amount of bread, cereals, potatoes, fruit and vegetables in your diet. Overall, your score in A must be lower than your score in B.

Section B

1 How many slices of bread (or equivalent) do you eat most days?
- **a** 5 or more
- **b** 2–4
- **c** 1 or fewer

2 How often do you eat rice or pasta in a week?
- **a** 5 or more times
- **b** 2–4 times
- **c** Sometimes or never

3 How many potatoes (the size of an egg) do you usually have at a meal?
- **a** 5 or more
- **b** 2–4
- **c** 1 or fewer

4 How many times a week do you eat cereal for breakfast?
- **a** 5 or more times
- **b** 2–4 times
- **c** Sometimes or never

5 How many portions of fruit and vegetables do you eat every day?
- **a** 5 or more
- **b** 2–4
- **c** 1 or fewer

chips

crisps

burger

potato

fruit

vegetables

Lesson 2: Reading review (1)

Ⓐ Which is the odd one out? Why?

1	apples	potatoes	lemons	oranges
2	meat	juice	tea	coffee
3	chocolate	pasta	cake	sweets
4	ice-cream	butter	cheese	rice
5	potatoes	eggs	crisps	chips
6	carrots	peas	cabbage	chicken

Ⓑ You are going to read an article about healthy eating. Read the title. Which of these sentences do you expect to find in the text? Tick one or more. Explain your answers.

1 ☐ Don't drink anything while you are eating.
2 ☐ Eat something before you go shopping.
3 ☐ I had a good meal in a restaurant last week.
4 ☐ I love eating burger and chips.
5 ☐ I will try to eat in a more healthy way in future.
6 ☐ You must eat many different kinds of food each week.
7 ☐ You should eat fruit every day.
8 ☐ Your body slows down at night.

Ⓒ Can you guess some of the advice? Cover the section headings. Make a list of *dos* (things you should do) and *don'ts* (things you should not do).

Ⓓ Uncover the section headings.
1 Which section will contain each of your pieces of advice?
2 What advice will the other sections contain?
3 Do you find any of the section headings strange?

Ⓔ You are going to read the text on page 22 of the Reading Resources book. Work in pairs.

The Dos and Don'ts of Healthy Eating

- Eat breakfast
- Eat snacks
- Drink water
- Think FAT!
- Eat a variety of foods

- Don't shop when you are hungry
- Don't eat in front of the TV
- Don't give up foods
- Don't starve
- Don't drink *and* eat

Student A
1 Read the dos.
2 Give the advice to your partner.

Student B
1 Read the don'ts.
2 Give the advice to your partner.

Ⓕ Work in the same pairs. Compare the advice in the two sections. Is any of the advice the same or similar in each section?

Ⓖ Which advice do you think is …
1 good?   2 strange?   3 stupid?

Lesson 3: Reading review (2)

A In this course you have learnt to deal with new words.

  1 Find and underline in the text the words in the yellow box.

  2 Is each word a noun, verb or adjective?

  3 Work out the meaning from context.

hungry	fatty	reduce
speeds up	saturated	starving
snacks	nutrients	stores
fuller	junk	chew

B In this course you have learnt to predict content from headings. Look at each section heading below. Find the topic sentence for that section.

C In this course you have learnt to understand the point of topic sentences. For each topic sentence in the table below, find the next sentence in the paragraph.

D In this course you have learnt about pronoun and adverb reference. What does each of these words refer to in the text on page 22 of the Reading Resources book?

  1 It (line 5) _____

  2 them (line 20) _____

  3 there (line 33) _____

  4 it (line 36) _____

  5 it (line 41) _____

  6 It (line 52) _____

Section headings	Topic sentences	Next sentences
Eat breakfast	Don't drink anything while you are eating.	Eat healthy, low-fat snacks between meals.
Eat snacks	Eat something before you go shopping.	*Frequency*
Drink water	Even if you are not very hungry, eat something.	Have a piece of bread or fruit.
Think FAT!	Firstly, you will enjoy your meal better.	If you don't, you will buy a chocolate bar or some junk food while you are there.
Eat a variety of foods	If you don't eat anything for several hours, you will eat much more at the next meal.	It is strange but true – well, almost!
Don't shop when you are hungry	If you like a particular food a lot, carry on eating it.	It will make you chew for longer.
Don't eat in front of the TV	Starving makes you fat.	Reduce the portions or the number of times you eat the food each week.
Don't give up foods	When you want to eat fatty foods, think about three things:	Secondly, you will take longer to eat it, and that is good for your body.
Don't starve	Drink at least two glasses of water after your meal.	That means you must eat many different kinds of food each week.
Don't drink *and* eat	Your body needs more than 40 different nutrients for good health.	You will feel fuller and not go back for seconds.

Lesson 4: Reading review (3)

A Match the dos and the don'ts of healthy eating.
1 Don't eat in front of the TV.
2 Don't give up foods.
3 Don't starve yourself.
4 Don't eat the same foods all the time.
5 Don't shop when you are hungry.
6 Don't drink water while you are eating.

a Drink water after you finish eating.
b Eat healthy snacks between meals.
c Go shopping after a meal.
d Have a variety of foods.
e Reduce the amount that you eat.
f Sit at a table.

B You are going to read a second article about healthy eating. Look at the heading and subheading. What will the main idea of this article be?

C Look at the section headings. Choose one section for each of these sentences and phrases from the text. Explain your choices.
1 Go to the shops regularly …
2 You get home at three o'clock and you're starving.
3 … plan to have 10-minute meals.
4 You are a complete failure, aren't you?
5 You must make an eating plan …
6 You plan a healthy meal, but it's complicated.
7 You plan to eat in a healthy way, then something goes wrong.
8 You shouldn't use meals in restaurants as an excuse for bad eating habits.

D Read the text on page 23 of the Reading Resources book. Check your answers to Exercises B and C.

E What does each of these pronouns and adverbs refer to?
1 Then (line 3)
2 there (line 5)
3 Then (line 9)
4 It (line 10)
5 it (line 19)
6 it (line 26)
7 them (line 29)
8 them (line 32)
9 then (line 37)

F Copy and complete Table 1.

Table 1: *How to plan for healthy eating*

	The problems	The solutions
1	no healthy things in the fridge	go shopping regularly; buy healthy things
2		
3		
4		
5		

THEME 1
Education, Student Life

answer (*n* and *v*)

ask (*v*)

begin (*v*)

dictionary (*n*)

end (*v*)

explain (*v*)

history (*n*)

learn (*v*)

listen (*v*)

mathematics (*n*)

question (*n*)

read (*v*)

right (*adj*)

science (*n*)

spell (*v*)

student (*n*)

study (*v*)

teach (*v*)

test (*n* and *v*)

university (*n*)

write (*v*)

wrong (*adj*)

advice (*n*)

advisor (*n*)

assignment (*n*)

consider (*v*)

instructor (*n*)

intelligence (*n*)

polite (*adj*)

relax (*v*)

respect (*n* and *v*)

THEME 2
Daily Life, Making the Most of It

afternoon (*n*)

autumn (*n*)

day (*n*)

evening (*n*)

first (*adj*)

hour (*n*)

last (*adj*)

late (*adj*)

later (*adj*)

midnight (*n*)

minute (*n*)

month (*n*)

morning (*n*)

night (*n*)

noon (*n*)

now (*adv*)

o'clock (*adv*)

past (*n* and *adv*)

quarter (*n*)

spring (*n*)

summer (*n*)

time (*n*)

today (*n*)

tomorrow (*n*)

tonight (*n*)

week (*n*)

winter (*n*)

year (*n*)

yesterday (*n*)

break (*n*)

on time

regular (*adj*)

regularly (*adv*)

social life (*n*)

spend (*v*)

weekend (*n*)

weekly (*adv*)

THEME 3
Work and Business, Are You Young and Energetic?

company (*n*)

computer (*n*)

desk (*n*)

e-mail (*n*)

envelope (*n*)

factory (*n*)

file (*n*)

job (*n*)

letter (*n*)

manager (*n*)

office (*n*)

secretary (*n*)

shelf / shelves (*n*)

shop (*n*)

start (*v*)

supermarket (*n*)

typist (*n*)

website (*n*)

work (*n* and *v*)

working hours (*n*)

benefit (*n*)

career (*n*)

employ (*v*)

employable (*adj*)

employee (*n*)

employer (*n*)

employment (*n*)

experience (*n*)

qualification (*n*)

requirement (*n*)

THEME 4
Science and Nature, Why Is It So Hot?

black (*adj*)

blue (*adj*)

brown (*adj*)

cloud (*n*)

cold (*adj*)

colour (*n* and *v*)

flower (*n*)

fog (*n*)

forest (*n*)

grass (*n*)

green (*adj*)

grey (*adj*)

hot (*adj*)

island (*n*)

lake (*n*)

mountain (*n*)

orange (*adj*)

rain (*n* and *v*)

red (*adj*)

river (*n*)

sea (*n*)

sky (*n*)

snow (*n* and *v*)

sun (*n*)

temperature (*n*)

thunderstorm (*n*)

tree (*n*)

water (*n*)

weather (*n*)

white (*adj*)

wind (*n*)

yellow (*adj*)

column (*n*)

latitude (*n*)

longitude (*n*)

meridian (*n*)

pole (*n*)

row (*n*)

source (*n*)

the Earth (*n*)

the Equator (*n*)

THEME 5
The Physical World, Big Country, Small Country

behind (prep)

between (prep)

corner (n)

country (n)

east (n)

in front of (prep)

in the centre of (prep)

island (n)

lake (n)

left (n)

mountain (n)

near (prep)

next to (prep)

north (n)

opposite (prep)

right (n)

river (n)

sea (n)

south (n)

town (n)

west (n)

compass (n)

landscape (n)

latitude (n)

location (n)

longitude (n)

region (n)

the Middle East (n)

THEME 6
Culture and Civilization, Fireworks, Horses and Bulls

adult (n)

age (n)

be born (v)

boy (n)

child (n)

congratulations (n)

dead (adj)

die (v)

family (n)

friend (n)

girl (n)

group (n)

guest (n)

live (v)

man (n)

married (adj)

name (n)

old (adj)

party (n)

people (n)

person (n)

present (n)

single (adj)

thank (v)

thank you (interj)

woman (n)

celebrate (v)

event (n)

happen (v)

prepare (v)

special (adj)

take place (v)

traditional (adj)

THEME 7
They Made Our World, A Brief History of Space Travel

accident (n)

airport (n)

arrive (v)

bicycle (n)

boat (n)

bus (n)

bus stop (n)

car (n)

come (v)

drive (v)

driver (n)

fly (v)

go (v)

land (v)

leave (v)

passenger (n)

pilot (n)

plane (n)

road (n)

sail (v)

sailor (n)

ship (n)

street (n)

take off (v)

traffic (n)

train (n)

planet (n)

satellite (n)

solar system (n)

space (n)

star (n)

the Earth (n)

the moon (n)

the sun (n)

THEME 8
Art and Literature, Romeo and Macbeth

bring (v)

build (v)

carry (v)

check (v)

climb (v)

come (v)

do (v)

draw (v)

end (v)

feel (v)

find (v)

get (v)

give (v)

go (v)

leave (v)

live (v)

look (v)

make (v)

meet (v)

move (v)

point (v)

put (v)

run (v)

say (v)

send (v)

start (v)

stop (v)

take (v)

talk (v)

tell (v)

walk (v)

want (v)

character (n)

comedy (n)

history (n)

literature (n)

play (n)

playwright (n)

tragedy (n)

THEME 9
Sports and Leisure, Can You Play Four Army Groups?

ball *(n)*

beach *(n)*

film *(n and v)*

football *(n)*

hobby *(n)*

magazine *(n)*

news *(n)*

newspaper *(n)*

play *(n and v)*

programme *(n)*

radio *(n)*

show *(n)*

sport *(n)*

sports *(n)*

swimming *(n)*

tennis *(n)*

theatre *(n)*

turn off *(v)*

turn on *(v)*

watch *(v)*

game *(n)*

land *(v)*

objective *(n)*

piece *(n)*

player *(n)*

turn *(n)*

THEME 10
Nutrition and Health, Eat, Drink and Be Healthy

bottle *(n)*

bread *(n)*

breakfast *(n)*

butter *(n)*

cheese *(n)*

chicken *(n)*

coffee *(n)*

cup *(n)*

drink *(n and v)*

eat *(v)*

egg *(n)*

fish *(n)*

food *(n)*

fruit *(n)*

glass *(n)*

ice-cream *(n)*

jam *(n)*

juice *(n)*

meal *(n)*

meat *(n)*

menu *(n)*

milk *(n)*

restaurant *(n)*

rice *(n)*

salad *(n)*

salt *(n)*

sandwich *(n)*

sugar *(n)*

tea *(n)*

vegetable *(n)*

biscuit *(n)*

burger *(n)*

cake *(n)*

cereal *(n)*

chip *(n)*

chocolate *(n)*

crisp *(n)*

pasta *(n)*

potato(es) *(n)*

sweet *(n)*

accident *(n)*

adult *(n)*

advice *(n)*

advisor *(n)*

afternoon *(n)*

age *(n)*

airport *(n)*

answer *(n and v)*

arrive *(v)*

ask *(v)*

assignment *(n)*

autumn *(n)*

ball *(n)*

baseball *(n)*

be born *(v)*

beach *(n)*

begin *(v)*

behind *(prep)*

benefit *(n)*

between *(prep)*

bicycle *(n)*

biscuit *(n)*

black *(adj)*

blue *(adj)*

boat *(n)*

bottle *(n)*

boy *(n)*

bread *(n)*

break *(n)*

breakfast *(n)*

bring *(v)*

brown *(adj)*

build *(v)*

burger *(n)*

bus *(n)*

bus stop *(n)*

butter *(n)*

cake *(n)*

car *(n)*

career *(n)*

carry *(v)*

celebrate *(v)*

cereal *(n)*

character *(n)*

check *(v)*

cheese *(n)*

chicken *(n)*

child *(n)*

chip *(n)*

chocolate *(n)*

climb *(v)*

cloud *(n)*

coffee *(n)*

cold *(adj)*

colour *(n and v)*

column *(n)*

come *(v)*

comedy *(n)*

company *(n)*

compass *(n)*

computer *(n)*

congratulations *(n)*

consider *(v)*

corner *(n)*

country *(n)*

crisp *(n)*

cup (n)	find (v)	island (n)	meridian (n)
day (n)	first (adj)	jam (n)	midnight (n)
dead (adj)	flower (n)	job (n)	milk (n)
dentist (n)	fly (v)	juice (n)	minute (n)
desk (n)	fog (n)	lake (n)	month (n)
dictionary (n)	food (n)	land (v)	morning (n)
die (v)	football (n)	land (v)	mountain (n)
die (v)	forest (n)	landscape (n)	move (v)
do (v)	friend (n)	last (adj)	move (v)
draw (v)	fruit (n)	late (adj)	name (n)
drink (n and v)	game (n)	later (adj)	near (prep)
drive (v)	get (v)	latitude (n)	news (n)
driver (n)	girl (n)	latitude (n)	newspaper (n)
east (n)	give (v)	learn (v)	next to (prep)
eat (n)	glass (n)	leave (v)	night (n)
egg (n)	go (v)	left (n)	noon (n)
e-mail (n)	grass (n)	letter (n)	north (n)
employ (v)	green (adj)	listen (v)	now (adj)
employable (adj)	grey (adj)	literature (n)	objective (n)
employee (n)	group (n)	live (v)	o'clock (adv)
employer (n)	guest (n)	location (n)	office (n)
employment (n)	happen (v)	longitude (n)	old (adj)
end (v)	history (n)	look (v)	on time (prep)
envelope (n)	history (n)	magazine (n)	opposite (prep)
evening (n)	hobby (n)	make (v)	orange (adj)
event (n)	hot (adj)	man (n)	party (n)
experience (n)	hour (n)	manager (n)	passenger (n)
explain (v)	ice-cream (n)	married (adj)	past (adv and n)
factory (n)	in front of (prep)	mathematics (n)	pasta (n)
family (n)	in the centre	meal (n)	people (n)
feel (v)	of (prep)	meat (n)	person (n)
file (n)	instructor (n)	meet (v)	piece (n)
film (n and v)	intelligence (n)	menu (n)	pilot (n)

plane (n)

planet (n)

play (n and v)

play (n and v)

player (n)

playwright (n)

point (v)

pole (n)

polite (adj)

potato(es) (n)

prepare (v)

present (n)

programme (n)

put (v)

qualification (n)

quarter (n)

question (n)

radio (n)

rain (n and v)

read (v)

red (adj)

region (n)

regular (adj)

regularly (adv)

relax (v)

requirement (n)

respect (n)

restaurant (n)

rice (n)

right (adj)

river (n)

road (n)

row (n)

run (v)

sail (v)

sailor (n)

salad (n)

salt (n)

sandwich (n)

satellite (n)

say (v)

science (n)

sea (n)

secretary (n)

send (v)

shelf / shelves (n)

ship (n)

shop (n)

show (n)

single (adj)

sky (n)

snow (n and v)

social life (n)

solar system (n)

source (n)

south (n)

space (n)

special (adj)

spell (v)

spend (v)

sport (n)

sports (n)

spring (n)

star (n)

start (v)

stop (v)

street (n)

student (n)

study (v)

sugar (n)

summer (n)

sun (n)

supermarket (n)

sweet (n)

swimming (n)

take off (v)

take place (v)

talk (v)

tea (n)

teach (v)

tell (v)

temperature (n)

tennis (n)

test (n and v)

thank (v)

thank you (interj)

the Earth (n)

the Equator (n)

the Middle East (n)

the moon (n)

the sun (n)

theatre (n)

thunderstorm (n)

time (n)

today (n)

tomorrow (n)

tonight (n)

town (n)

traditional (adj)

traffic (n)

tragedy (n)

train (n)

tree (n)

turn (n)

turn off (v)

turn on (v)

typist (n)

university (n)

vegetable (n)

walk (v)

want (v)

watch (v)

water (n)

weather (n)

website (n)

week (n)

weekend (n)

weekly (adv)

west (n)

white (adj)

wind (n)

winter (n)

woman (n)

work (n and v)

working hours (n)

write (v)

wrong (adj)

year (n)

yellow (adj)